GOOPS
AND HOW TO BE THEM

GOOPS

AND HOW TO BE THEM

A Manual of Manners for Polite Infants
Inculcating many Juvenile Virtues
Both by Precept and Example
With Ninety Drawings

By GELETT BURGESS

Applewood Books
Bedford, Massachusetts

Goops and How To Be Them
was originally published in 1900.

Thank you for purchasing an Applewood Book.
Applewood reprints America's lively
classics—books from the past that are still
of interest to modern readers.
For a free copy of our current catalog, write to:
Applewood Books
P.O. Box 365
Bedford, MA 01730.

ISBN 1-55709-392-X

Library of Congress Control Number: 2003107213

To Agnes
who is
Not
(always)
a Goop!

TABLE OF CONTENTS

TABLE OF CONTENTS

Of these Rhymes, ten first appeared in
"St. Nicholas," *and are here reprinted
by permission of the* Century Company

INTRODUCTION

LET me introduce a Race
Void of Beauty and of Grace,
Extraordinary Creatures
With a Paucity of Features.
Though their Forms are fashioned ill,
They have Manners stranger still;
For in Rudeness they're Precocious,
They're Atrocious, they're Ferocious!
Yet you'll learn, if you are Bright,
Politeness from the Impolite.
When you've finished with the Book,
At your Conduct take a Look;
Ask yourself, upon the Spot,
Are you Goop, or are you Not?
For, although it's Fun to See them
It is TERRIBLE to Be them!

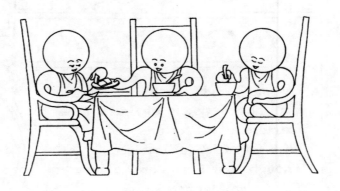

TABLE MANNERS.—I.

THE Goops they lick their fingers,
  And the Goops they lick their
        knives;
They spill their broth on the table-
        cloth—
  Oh, they lead disgusting lives!
The Goops they talk while eating,
  And loud and fast they chew;
And that is why I'm glad that I
  Am not a Goop—are you?

TABLE MANNERS. — II.

THE Goops are gluttonous and rude,
They gug and gumble with their food;
They throw their crumbs upon the floor,
And at dessert they tease for more;
They will not eat their soup and bread
But like to gobble sweets, instead,
And this is why I oft decline,
When I am asked to stay and dine!

CLEANLINESS

THE Goops they are spotted on chin and on cheek,
   You could dig the dirt off with a trowel!
But *you* wash your face twenty times every week,
   And you don't do it *all* with the towel!

The Goops are all dirty, and what do they do?
   They like to be dirty, and stay so.
But if *you* were dirty, you'd wash, wouldn't you?
   If you needed a bath, you would say so!

NEATNESS

Goops leave traces every-
    where—
Gum stuck underneath the
    chair,
Muddy footprints in the
    hall,
Show that Goops have been
    to call;
Shoes and stockings on the
    floor
Show where Goops have
    been before!

COURTESY

I wonder why it is polite
In shaking hands, to give your *right*.
I wonder why it is refined
In passing one, to go *behind*.
I wonder why it is well-bred,
If you must sneeze, to turn your head.
Perhaps the reason is because
The Goops, they never have such laws!

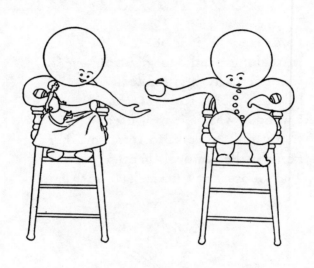

GENEROSITY

WHEN you have candy, do you go
And give your sister half?
When little brother stubs his toe,
Do you look on and laugh?

The greediest Goop would give away
The things he didn't need —
To share the toys with which you play,
That's generous, indeed!

CONSIDERATION

When you're old, and get to be
Thirty-four or forty-three,
Don't you hope that you will see
   Children all respect you?

Will they, without being told,
   Wait on you, when you are old,
     Or be heedless, selfish, cold?
      I *hope* they'll not neglect
        you!

MISS MANNERS

No matter how you
wish
For the last one on the
dish,
Miss Manners has a right
to it, not you;
And the largest one of all,
Or the nicest, big or small—
Well, I think you'd better
leave her *that* one too!

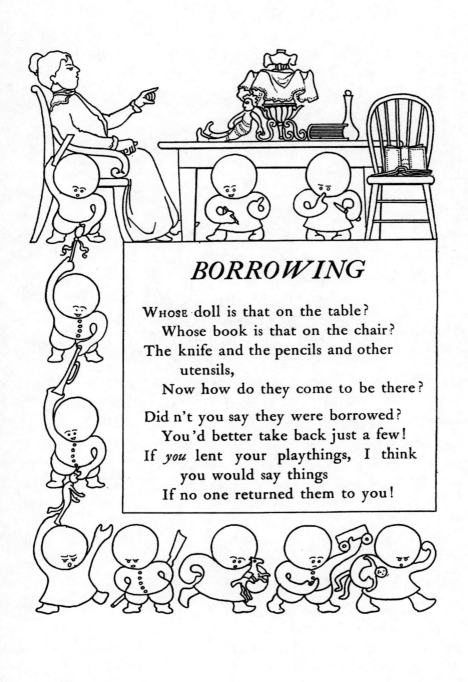

BORROWING

Whose doll is that on the table?
　　Whose book is that on the chair?
The knife and the pencils and other
　　　utensils,
　　Now how do they come to be there?

Did n't you say they were borrowed?
　　You'd better take back just a few!
If *you* lent your playthings, I think
　　　you would say things
　　If no one returned them to you!

MEMORY

My teacher taught me, yesterday,
A very pretty piece to say;
But when I try to think of it,
I can't remember it a bit!
My head's so full of toys and such,
I can't remember very much!

My teacher told me yesterday
"*Work when you work;*
Play when you play!"
When I am playing with my toys
I am the busiest of boys;
But when I study or I work
I'm 'fraid I *am* inclined to shirk!

BOOKS

I have a notion
    The Books on the shelves
Are just as much persons
    As we are, ourselves.

When you are older,
    You'll find this is true;
You'd better be careful
    To make Books like you!

HONESTY

THE boy who plays at marbles and does n't try to cheat,
Who always keeps his temper, no matter if he 's beat,
Is sure to be a favorite with all upon the street.

The girl who counts her hundreds very fairly, when she 's "it"
Who does n't peep or listen, nor turn around a bit,
I 'm sure she 's not a Goop, in fact, she 's quite the opposite!

"*WHY?*"

Josephus never yet was heard
To say but just one single word!
When father said to go to bed,
Then "*Why?*" was all Josephus said.
When mother bade him stop his play,
Then "*Why?*" Josephus used to say.
He always made the same reply.
'T was never anything but
"WHY?"

BED-TIME

THE night is different from the day —
It's darker in the night;
How can you ever hope to play
When it's no longer light?

When bed-time comes, it's time for you
To stop, for when you're yawning,
You should be dreaming what you'll do
When it's to-morrow morning.

MODESTY

THE proper time for you to show
Whatever little tricks you know
Is when grown people ask you to;
Then you may show what you
can do!
But sometimes mother's head
will ache
With all the jolly noise you make,
And sometimes other people, too,
Can't spend the time to play
with you!

DISFIGURATION

HAVE you ever seen the scrawls
On the fences and the walls,
All the horrid little pictures and the horrid
little names?
Don't you think it is a shame?
Are the Goops the ones to blame?
Did you ever catch them playing at their
horrid little games?

BRAVERY

It's terrible brave
To try to save
A girl on a runaway horse;
You could do that, of course!
But think of trying
To keep from crying,
When you're hungry and tired
and cross—
You couldn't do *that*,
of course!

TIDINESS

LITTLE scraps of paper,
  Little crumbs of food,
Make a room untidy,
  Everywhere they're
    strewed.

Do you sharpen pencils,
  Ever, on the floor?
What becomes of orange-
    peels
And your apple-core?

Can you blame your mother
  If she looks severe,
When she says, "It looks
    to me
As if the Goops were
    here"?

PATIENce

THE clock will go slow
If you watch it, you know;
    You must work right along
      and forget it.
So study your best
Till it's time for a rest,
    The clock will go fast, if you
      let it!

FORTITUDE

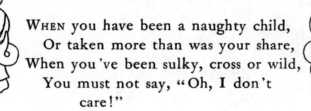

WHEN you have been a naughty child,
   Or taken more than was your share,
When you've been sulky, cross or wild,
   You must not say, "Oh, I don't
      care!"

But when you hate to see it rain,
   And when it's time to comb your hair,
And when you have a little pain,
   Then you can say, "Oh, I don't care!"

GEORGE ADOLPHUS

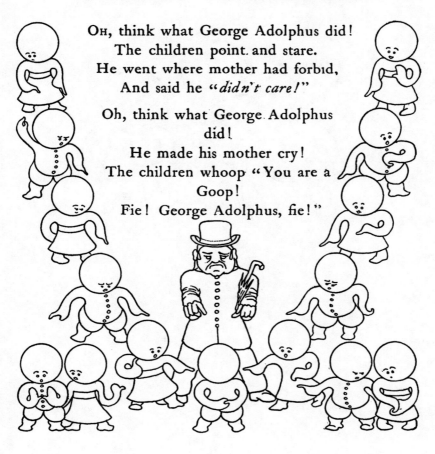

Oh, think what George Adolphus did!
The children point and stare.
He went where mother had forbid,
And said he *"didn't care!"*

Oh, think what George Adolphus
did!
He made his mother cry!
The children whoop "You are a
Goop!
Fie! George Adolphus, fie!"

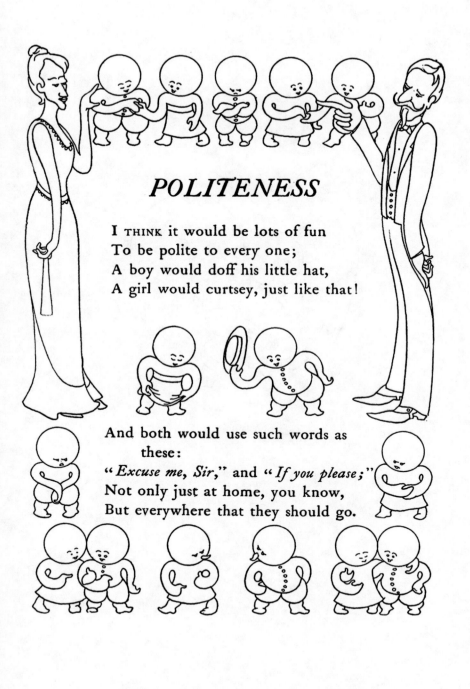

POLITENESS

I THINK it would be lots of fun
To be polite to every one;
A boy would doff his little hat,
A girl would curtsey, just like that!

And both would use such words as
these:
"*Excuse me, Sir,*" and "*If you please;*"
Not only just at home, you know,
But everywhere that they should go.

GENTLENESS

WHEN you are playing with
the girls,
You must not pull their
pretty curls;
If you are gentle when
you play,
You will be glad of it
some day.

HOSPITALITY

When a person visits you, remember he's your guest,
Receive him very kindly, and be sure he has the best;
Make him very comfortable and show him all your toys,
And only play the games you're very sure that he enjoys.

When you pay a visit, never grumble or complain,
Try to be so affable they'll want you there again;
Don't forget the older ones, your hostess least of all,
When you're leaving tell her you have had a pleasant call!

PETS

ALMOST every Goop forgets
When it's time to feed his pets,
   'Cause his memory fails;

Listen to his wails!
He is often scratched or bitten
By the puppy or the kitten,
   'Cause he pulls their tails!

REMEMBER

REMEMBER not to suck your thumb;
Remember not to slam the door;
Remember when the callers come
To take your toys from off the floor.

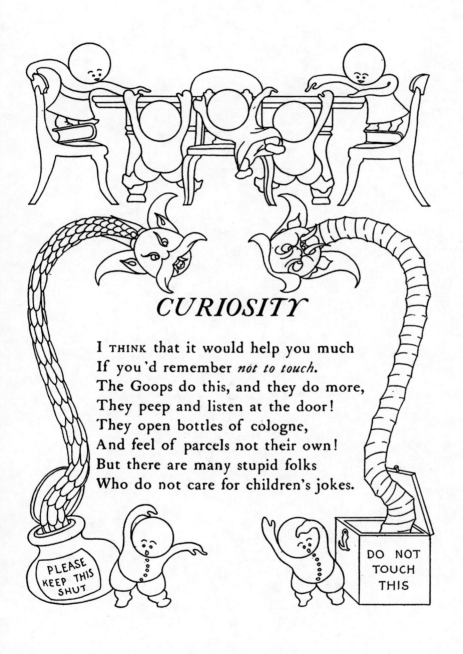

CURIOSITY

I THINK that it would help you much
If you'd remember *not to touch*.
The Goops do this, and they do more,
They peep and listen at the door!
They open bottles of cologne,
And feel of parcels not their own!
But there are many stupid folks
Who do not care for children's jokes.

PLEASE
KEEP THIS
SHUT

DO NOT
TOUCH
THIS

WILLY

WILLY broke the window-
    pane.
Willy spilled the ink,
Willy left the water-pipe
    Running in the sink!

Did his mother punish him?
    No! I'll tell you why.
Willy, he owned up to it,
    And didn't tell a lie!

Willy told his mother
    Before she found it out
He said: "I am so sorry!"
    She said "I have no doubt!"

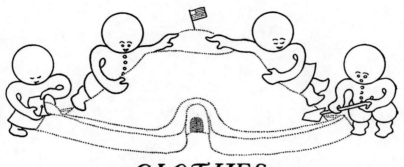

CLOTHES

When you are playing in the dirt,
You should wear clothes you cannot hurt;
It will not matter, when they're worn,
If they are just a *little* torn.

But when you're really nicely dressed,
Be careful of your Sunday Best!
You must not crawl upon your knees;
Be careful of your elbows, please!

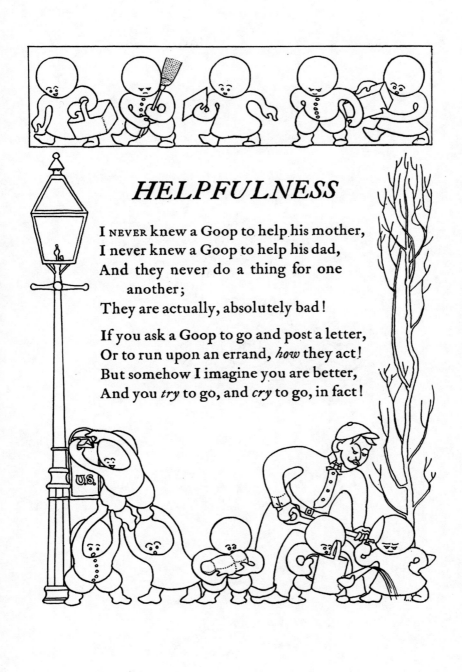

HELPFULNESS

I NEVER knew a Goop to help his mother,
I never knew a Goop to help his dad,
And they never do a thing for one
  another;
They are actually, absolutely bad!

If you ask a Goop to go and post a letter,
Or to run upon an errand, *how* they act!
But somehow I imagine you are better,
And you *try* to go, and *cry* to go, in fact!

QUIETNESS

Hush! for your father is reading.
Hush! for your mother is ill.
  Hush! for the baby
  Is sleeping, and may be
He'll catch a nice dream if you're still.
Kiss me, and promise you will!

ORDER

Make your soldiers march away,
When you're finished with your
    play.
Lead them to the barrack-box,
Make them carry all your blocks.
Teach your doll to go to bed,
Not to lie about instead;
Tell her she must clear away
Everything she's used to-day.
All your playthings and your toys
Must be trained like girls and boys!

TEASING

Tease to linger longer when your mother bids you go;
Tease to have a penny when your father answers, "No!"
Tease to have a story when your uncle doesn't please;
That's the way to be a Goop—*tease, tease, tease!*

Hint about the carriage when there's only room for three;
Hint about the toys you like and every doll you see;
    Hint about the candy, say you're fond
        of peppermint;
    That's the way to be a Goop—*hint,*
      hint, hint!

INTERRUPTION

Don't interrupt your father when he's telling
funny jokes;
Don't interrupt your mother when she's
entertaining folks;
Don't interrupt the visitors when they have
come to call,—
In fact, it's generally wiser
not to interrupt at all.

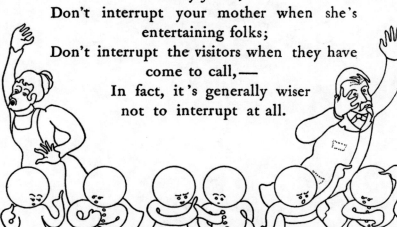

CRY-BABY

I'M sure that I would rather die
Than have my playmates see me cry;
It twists your face
And knots your forehead,
And makes you look all cross and
horrid;
And every one who sees you cries
"What *is* the matter with your
eyes?"

CAUTION

WHEN you travel in the street,
Are you cautious and discreet?
Do you look about for horses
When your little brother crosses?
Do you go the shortest way,
Never stopping once to play?

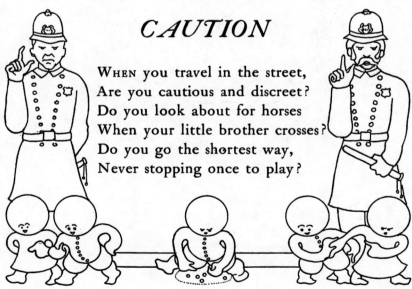

TARDINESS

GOODNESS gracious sakes alive!
Mother said, "Come home at five!"
Now the clock is striking six,
I am in a norful fix!
She will think I can't be trusted,
And she'll say that she's disgusted!

OBEDIENCE

THE Goops are very hard to
kill,
So they hang out the Window-sill;
Down the Banisters they slide —
I could do it if I tried;
But when Mother tells me "don't,"
Then, of course
I really won't!

CHURCH HEADACHES

When 't is time to go to church
  Do you ever have a chill?
When 't is time to go to school,
  Do you fancy you are ill?
Oh, be very cautious, please,
I can tell by signs like these
You have got the Goop Disease!

PERSEVERANCE

Tony started bright and early, clearing up his room,
Soon he found he had to stop and make a little broom;

So then he went into the yard to get a little stick,
But the garden needed weeding, so he set about it, quick!

Then he found his wagon he intended to repair,
So he went into the cellar for the hammer that was there;

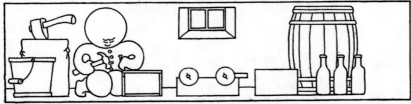

He'd just begun to build a box, when it was time for dinner;
And that's why Tony's father called his son a *"good beginner."*

DOLL-TIME

SPRING's the time for marbles
   And Fall's the time for tops,
But boys don't know, they only go
   By seeing them in shops!

They like a sled in Winter,
   In Summer 't is a kite;
But dolls are found the whole year
     round
   And every day and night!

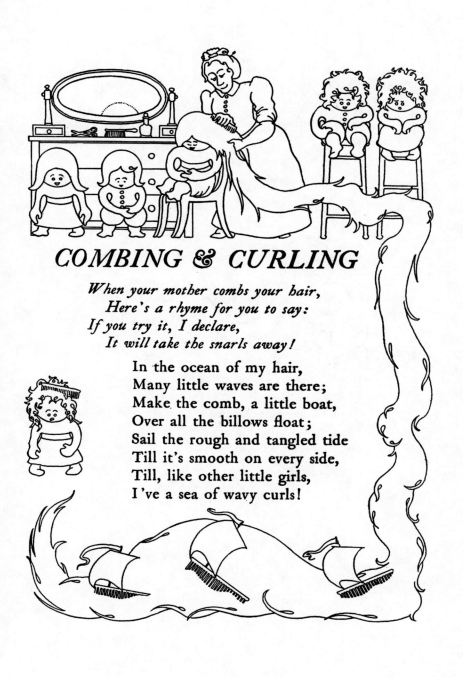

COMBING & CURLING

When your mother combs your hair,
Here's a rhyme for you to say:
If you try it, I declare,
It will take the snarls away!

In the ocean of my hair,
Many little waves are there;
Make the comb, a little boat,
Over all the billows float;
Sail the rough and tangled tide
Till it's smooth on every side,
Till, like other little girls,
I've a sea of wavy curls!

CHEERFULNESS

Now the book is finished
    (It's too long by half,
      Mere didactic chaff),
One more rule won't hurt you:
When you practise Virtue,
    Do it with a laugh!